IS YOUR LIFE MEANINGFUL?

FOR A BETTER LIFESTYLE

MANOHAR LAL SHARMA

From going through all topics enshrined in nut shell but complete in all respects, touching all corners of life including past and present, one come to the conclusion that, writer has depicted somewhat real picture of the prevailing circumstances some of the topic which reflects the mirror of the present society. The writer has beautifully made use of metaphors, similes and catharses, thereby attempt has been made to suggest some positive changes in the existing society. Some other topics touched by the writer suggest the ways heading towards" Moksha" which is the ultimate aim of Manush Jeevan". Stress has been shown on the adoption of good deeds which ultimately transform the ill society into a healthy society for the betterment of human life.

Contents

Contents

Foreword

This book has touched topics which are concerning environment in general and life in particular. A few of them are experience based, whereas other contain view and have reference to religious teaching.

Values are being ignored and eroded in the present age. Man has become self-centric and commercial. People rest expectations and believe on give and take. Can we live a meaningful life in the present atmosphere? Life is very stressful these days, everyone is busy in making money, running for his life, generating lifestyle leaving behind all the thoughts and beliefs that are useful for a person to live a happy and meaningful life. Therefore, an attempt has been made by the author to bring out them in brief by this book as most of us don't have time and habit to sit for a longer spell. Effort has been made to abstain from controversial writing. In case there are any hints appearing detrimental to a faith, religion, community or profession be assumed as coincidence and given a broader thought.

About The Author

Manohar Lal Sharma, born on April 30 1944, in Chhatra village (Now in POK), embarked on a remarkable journey shaped by his rural upbringing, military service, and spiritual beliefs. Despite completing his secondary education in a government school, his passion for reading and writing was undeniable. However, destiny led him to join the Indian Army as a sepoy, where he served diligently across various regions of the country for approximately 28 years, retiring with the rank of Subedar Major (Captain). Throughout his life, Sharma's spiritual inclinations, nurtured by his family environment, remained a guiding force. Married at the age of 25 and blessed with children, he shouldered the responsibility of his family from a young age. After retiring from the army, Sharma pursued a career as an accountant at the SSP's office Poonch for about 14 years. Yet, his enduring love for literature persisted. Turning to writing as a means of expression, Sharma began documenting his thoughts and experiences on plain paper. Over time, these musings evolved into books. His writings, imbued with spiritual wisdom and reflections on karma, offer readers profound insights into the importance of righteous living and the power of good deeds. Through his works, Sharma emphasizes the significance of belief and moral integrity in navigating life's journey.

Acknowledgements

It's my pleasure that you honor my thoughts. I have touched topics which are concerning environment in general and life in particular. A few of them are experience based, whereas other contain view and have reference to religious teaching. Values are being ignored and eroded in the present age. Man has become self-centric and commercial. People rest expectations and believe on give and take. Can we live a meaningful life in the present atmosphere? Therefore, an attempt has been made to bring out them in brief as most of us don't have time and habit to sit for a longer spell. Effort has been made to abstain from controversial writing. In case there are any hints appearing detrimental to a faith, religion, community or profession be assumed as coincidence and given a broader thought. I shall be grateful if your valuable comments are made known to me either orally or through mail to mend. Hope you may like it.

ONE
SATISFACTION

By and large majority of us are far from satisfaction may be this is the reason that we are creative and are in the race of completion. In this material world every one is a competitor in different fields. One may feel comfortable after gaining prestige, women wealth and luxurious life but not satisfied. It is said that this race is so intense that one has no time to think of self. He works morning to evening, even late hours of night but feels un satisfied. However, the idea behind this race is to leave behind your brother, kinsmen or neighbor in different fields. The choice may vary from man to man. Believing in materialism may be found in women, food, wealth and prestige. Whereas sane persons may be in the race of acquiring knowledge, penance and giving donation etc. However, none of them feel satisfied. Dissatisfaction keeps us busy and we work in the same direction keeping in view the goal. To certain extent most of us know that the race of material world is endless and brings exhaustion, still no lesson is learnt People fond of prestige will always prefer to be in the lime light either in the print media columns or in the electronic media making speech, shaking hands with a leader or a high official. They are seen in religious congregation and condolence gathering at cremation grounds irrespective of caste creed and religion They remain busy from morning to evening and come home tired. They never question themselves what they have derived throughout the day Are they feel satisfied?

Similar is the state of persons desirous of women, wine, wealth and commodities bringing short lived enjoyment and tiredness for a longer spell They too know that their race is meaningless still they don't desist from indulging in it. Knowing fully pros and cons of a particular act, if indulged in a bad one repeatedly is a bad habit or addiction which is not beneficial in any form. It is far from satisfaction. Sane person believing in acquiring knowledge, penance and donation adopt the right way of living. Though they too remain devoid of satisfaction, still it like ocean and never comes to the brim. It never over flows. The more you acquire, the more you feel that there are many more things which could be known. It is said that a man approached a scholar on death bed with a question that how he feels about knowledge. The answer was that I an atom in the great desert. So, knowledge never ends. Penance is also endless. It requires lot of efforts, detachment from loved one and material world. Its main purpose is to achieve bliss, moksha or merger with the Supreme. Get rid of bondage of birth and death. At the same time, it requires lot of efforts to have concentration and devotion. For this one should have pious mann, wachan and karma. Concentration could be had with repeated Satsang`s, chanting of holy name, dhayana and above all with the grace of Almighty. Concentration is the first step to achieve devotion and finally reach the stage of bliss. Then only your penance flourish. Donation is the other way of storing good karmas which ultimately lead to liquidate bad one committed willfully or in advertently. One should therefore try to accumulate as many of them as possible and never feel satisfied with them. We have the tale of Raja Beli when committed to Bhavan avtar to donate three steps land, intervened by Guru Shukraraya that don't do this as the later knew that Bhavan Avtar is no one else then Bhagwan Vishnu. But the guru could not deter Raja Beli to rethink of the promise made to Bhavan Avtar. So, one should never feel satisfied with donation. In the same vein the great Politician "Chanakya" has said that "one should be satisfied with food, money and wife and never be satisfied with Knowledge, penance and donation." These are the right deeds to be performed by the human.

TWO

IF'S AND BUTS

We generally live in the age of ifs and buts. We are very quick in passing remarks on any happening or execution for example this should have been done in this way or that way. It would have happened like this or like that. Had I been there I would have tackled the problem this way or that way. Had he not gone on river bed he might have not been flown with the tide. This way most of us indulge in gossip or mental exercise which has no relevance to a particular situation. Though we know that it is useless, still we don't refrain this practice. We are lacking the habit of acceptance. We should cultivate the habit of acceptance. As most of us know that our actions are controlled by someone. We too know that "The limit of one's life, deeds, knowledge, money and death are decided when one comes in the womb." Behind every act we assume that we are the doers. But it is not true we the toys in the hands of the great master. We have to dance according to of the direction of the operator. We have to act only as the remote is elsewhere controlled by the someone. If we don't accept it will be like swimming against the tide. After a brief struggle we will feel tired and exhausted. Therefore, better accept the situation and act as directed. We forget that it is the game of karmas and controlled by a fool proof brain. HIS creation is fool proof. The operator leaves no scope of amendment, alteration or correction. It is said that Godliness begins where human brain ends. No human brain can change the cycle of seasons. No human brain can change the timing of rising and setting Sun. No human brain can check the increasing and decreasing system of Moon. No human brain can change the cycle of tides in the ocean. No human brain can either make or change the shape of an orange or can disturb the packing of pomegranate. No human made device can measure the fragrance in the flowers or can bridle the flow of air and so on. No human brain can change the destiny of a man as it is based on karmas. To be a king or cobbler is the game of karmas. The destiny could only be changed with pious karmas and with the blessing of the creator. Experience has shown that a father has a scholar son. Whereas his other son is a class IV employee. Both have taken birth in the same family but they bear different karmas and destiny. The scholar may be thin and class IV employee may be robust. They bear different physique. The scholar may be a miser, whereas the latter may be liberal. So, the destiny is karma based. Therefore, pleasures and pains are self-created or cultivated. Alteration if any could take place with karmas only. One should therefore concentrate on karma and should not indulge in mental exercise of ifs and buts or any happening. Instead act awakened and make sure that as many as pious karmas are accumulated in order to gain pleasure and live stress free and happy life. Besides he will have enough of saving of good karmas and will not have the fear of death and Yumyacthana (punishments of the hell). Instead of making ifs and buts he should let himself loose in the tide of environment and accept any happening cheerfully as anything happens, happens for good. Moreover no one is competent to stop or change it. It is the generator, operator and destroyer who holds the remote. We are the tools and puppets and toys in His hand. We have to comply only. It is said that "Rote rote hasna seikho and haste haste rona, Jitni chabi bheri Ram ne utna chale khilona." Surrender is the best way of living and a sort of prayer too.

THREE

DEATH KEEPS NO CALENDAR

Every day we find that people die irrespective of age group. But there is a belief in general that old people die, sick die, those meeting with un natural death die. Experience has shown that one has to die sooner or later. But our planning and action do not commensurate with so called thoughts that death is un predictable. Our actions are long lasting as if we have to stay here for a very long period. If not, we think of generations depending upon relations. In fact, there are no relations but is the game of karmas. Thinking of successive generations, we work over time to make them comfortable. At times it leads to evil doing and polluted actions. We work for kids and family members. A father who had a very tuff time during his child hood tries to give his son better life and makes sure that his son doesn't suffer. In some cases, this affection becomes excessive and instead of better grooming spoil the career of his son. To quote father lived in grass house and makes a pucca house for his son, acquires sufficient landed property through fair and foul means, the son in some cases feels comfortable and instead of adding to it becomes idle and non-creative. In the race of material world father works day and night and no time to sit with family members. Father being healthy has no fear of death. When body is healthy it seems that death is far but it is not true. We are known as aadami that is we are alive till next breath. If the breathing cycle stops, we are no more We should therefore assume that death and God are around us. God is watching our actions. Whereas the death is waiting for the time set by God. In the same

vein Chanakya has said "When body is healthy death seems far." But it is just an illusion, death always hovers around and can prick the bubble of life any time. So whatever good you know do it tomorrow will be late". Since death keeps no calendar, we should shun believing that only old people die, we should act awakened and make sure that our deeds are pious and we are not adding to bad karmas. We should derive minimum from this world. For example, if we need a twig brush, we should not cut whole branch of a tree. Similarly, if we can take bath with one bucket we shouldn't drain a drum of water from water tank. If we can survive with a chapati and vegetable we should not run after non vegetarian food. The goal of human life is the merger with the Supreme which is possible with sat karmas We are different from animals because of knowledge and freedom of thoughts and karmas. In case we are unable to achieve moksha, then at least we should elevate ourselves so that we may be placed in the category of devas. If that too is not possible, we should get a better birth in human life. But it often happens that we are placed in lower spices in most of the cases and therefore remain in the cycle of taking rebirth (chaurasi lakh yoni). So, it is imperative that we should always remember that death keeps no calendar and we should refrain from bad deeds. Act awakened and ensure that we are not adding to pap karmas. We should remain pure by mann, wachan and karma. Whatever good we know we should do it and not wait for tomorrow or additional knowledge about sat karmas."

Jane chale jate hein khan dunia se jane wale

FOUR

THE MEDIATOR

There is a tendency in general in order to be in good books or gain credit people say I did this or that when the outcome is pleasing or successful. I managed his service or rescued him from trouble and so on. They want to harvest credit in case things are favorable or going on well. If the things are going adverse no one will come forward to share the responsibility instead it will be thrown on others shoulders. Many ifs and buts play their role. To quote father says I groomed my son in a decent way by providing all necessities and luxuries to the possible extent thereby making him a successful man. But the executing end rests with son. He implemented as directed, obeyed and timely worked hard for better results. Who was at the helm, his karmas which paved way for his success. The father was the mediator at different stages to help him. Similarly, mother too at time say that she did a lot for her kid which is true to a large extent. She of course played a pivotal role in bringing him up. But in general, she never rests any expectations from son like father. The love of mother is natural and it has no comparison. She too is a mediator only. The son, however, has been placed in her lap because of karmas to equalize give and take process. In the same vein elder brother puts lot of efforts in the development of his younger brother. To quote his mother when she is at work and tells him to take care of the young one. He lifts him and tries to please him by offering toys etc to make him laugh in case he weeps. When he is hungry, he gives him baby milk and ensures that the baby is comfortable. He continues carrying him till he sleeps. In the process many a time the baby wets him too. The elder never minds instead accepts it with a smile. He contributes a lot in his capacity but he too is a mediator. To a certain extent neighbor too has a role in the development of a child. He may play with him, lift him give him toys and food etc. In his association the child may gain knowledge and enhance his education and so on. In certain cases, he arranges for him a good school and help in acquiring a job. He also plays a role of a mediator in the capacity of a neighbor. Kith and to help in grooming of an individual. They love him, teach, and feed him and so on. They take care of him during his stay as a guest in the home. They try to make him comfortable within the means they have. In case the child is promising, they will help him in his education and suggest various fields of progress by joining higher institutions. They act as mediator. Individual at his own because of past karmas choose and implement good advice at an opportune time which later paves way of his progress. In fact, the individual, doer has to play the main role in progress or ruin of one's life. He cuts whatever he had sown. Karmas are at the helm. Mediators can help up to 10% only. Rest all depends upon the actions of an individual. He elevates himself with pure thoughts, actions and company. His pleasant speech also helps in his progress. His present performance not only becomes admirable but he paves way for a better life in the coming costume. So far as his past karmas are concerned, they had been excellent due to which he was blessed with a body of a human which is the gate way of moksha. Therefore, the mediators are only helping hand.

FIVE

MAN IS KNOWN BY HIS ACTIONS

Most of us are aware of good or bad still we fail to bridle bad performance. We know that cigarette is injurious to health, but cannot contain smoking. Liquor too is harmful, but we are unable to refrain from it. To lie is a said to be a sin but we go on lying. There may be an array of examples which could be discussed. Any misdeed committed inadvertently could be forgiven but a misdeed committed willfully cannot be forgiven. Generally, our performance is based on our blood, grooming, education company and food we eat. It is said that men belonging to good families never dupe others till their last breath, that is why kings used to keep them in the courts as they were most reliable. Therefore, blood plays key role in one's performance. Pure is the blood, pure are the actions. So, it is imperative that purity of blood is maintained and heritage is not disturbed. Besides the culture of one wife as enshrined in Ramayana should be followed. One should remain faithful to her and eschew from acting as bull. The purity inherited from elders should be maintained at all costs. Then comes grooming of kids.

Those below the age of five years should be given love by all members of family so that they could prove themselves robust and courageous in their subsequent span of life. After this age their activities should be watched and in case of any wrong doing they should be admonished, if the situation demands be punished appropriately. This way they are to be acquainted with good or bad performance. This process should be continued till the age of 16 years. Elders too in the home should behave like gentlemen Their utterance and behavior should he well thought over so that right example is set. As regards education children should be given highest education to awaken them so that they could prove themselves good material for their parents in particular and society in general. If one fails to acquire higher education, he should be diverted towards religion. It is the knowledge and religion that separates him from rest of the creatures. Religion in fact makes the life meaningful. If one cultivates faith in religion, he can elevate himself and lives like a human. In fact, going by the religion should be the first choice. However, majority of us believe in material world and join the race of acquiring luxuries of life which remain s unquenched till last breath. Now a days education is gained to earn, acquire wealth and make the life comfortable to have name and fame. In this process doctors and teacher have committed themselves more and instead of living a planned life are running after wealth, thereby have no time for self. They live like a machine which is at the disposal of others. That is why it is said "Knowledge is Power". There is an adage that "a man is known by the company he keeps." Company plays a pivotal role in one's life. In our language people say "sekh na sekh gwandu sekh". You learn from your companions. You are bound to catch heat while playing with fire. A fisherman cannot evade wetting while fishing. You have to get spots while handling coal. If you are sitting amongst drunkards, nobody will say that you are taking milk. Bad company always spoils, whereas good company crystalize a man. It is said that a neem tree cannot become sweet if watered with milk and butter. Similarly wicked person cannot become pious even if dipped many a times in Holy Ganges. It is therefore imperative that one should keep good company. Food leaves a great impact on your thinking. It is said that "Jaisa khaye ann waisa bane mann" Once thinking is spoiled your actions will go accordingly. We should therefore go for vegetarian food and refrain from non-vegetarian; besides we should avoid intoxicants, smoking and other stuff containing tobacco. It is said that human body is like a temple which should be clean and tidy. Besides man is gifted with five senses and knowledge. Knowledge and religion separate us from other beings. Knowledge helps us to differentiate between good or bad. Points brought out above if kept in mind will definitely help us to live a life like human. A meaningful life and our stay in this planet will be remembered and cherished by the successive generations. Doesn't matter one fails to achieve bliss or moksha, but at least a memorable performance is enough and expected from each one of us.

SIX

AVOID DUAL ROLE

Experience has shown that most of us have two faces, two types of behavior, two type of action and so on. In the process one goes far from his origin. At times it becomes difficult to form an opinion about an individual. His identity becomes questionable. In some cases, individual himself remains in quandary to form an opinion about himself. The reason of his dual behavior is to remain in good books of public. Whereas in domestic life and actions in private depetic the real picture of his self. Therefore, it goes at par with the saying "Hathi ke dant khane ke aur dekhane ke aur". Though while acting so, he may deceive public to a certain extent but there remains a sign of humiliation in the core of heart. It is said that face is the index of mind. It shows a ray of gravity of self-confidence. By and large theory of people appears sound but there is a large gap in the general behavior and the origin of an individual. Probably the reason is, it is easy to comment but difficult to implement., In case they go by their origin or temperament their shortcomings are exposed and they cannot harvest good opinion of the masses. Therefore, every effort is made to keep theory acceptable in the eye of public. For example, it is always said and taught that one should be lucid and speak truth but most of fail to comply it sometimes depending upon the situation and place. Gandhi ji used to tell that life of a person should be like an open book. But at certain occasion one has to maintain secrecy in domestic and public life in case of rulers and belt forces secrecy is of immense importance and has to be maintained at all costs Thus one has to play dual role as an exception. However, with the above exception one can go by the saying and avoid dual role. He can act transparent and achieve perfection in this context. Acting original have many benefits One will be free from stress, strain and remain mentally calm. He will have less load on his brain and can concentrate on present and will be able to take quick decision at an opportune time. Acting original not only keep us mentally less committed but also enables us to cultivate a habit of living in present which is a great art. This leads to perfection in each and every sphere of life. Especially if you want to be religious and believe in 'Dhayana', Your concentration goes on enhancing and finally bring perfection. In case you are a workman or a skilled worker you will be whole hearty committed in it and produce a beautiful toy, idol, furniture item and so on. Besides if one remains committed with his job with core of heart it brings satisfaction which is a great achievement. Storing unwanted thoughts is a great hindrance in your decision making. Repenting on past and making future plans are uncalled for. Wise care for present and chart their actions. If at all one has to think for future, think for tomorrow only not for day after as death keeps no calendar. Therefore, one should act as he is and avoid dual role.

SEVEN
CAREER BUILDING

There is a saying that "one should never be so simple". Go to jungle and behold that only simple and straight trees have been cut down but those are haphazard type have been spared". This is true to a great extent in the present age. But to go by the saying in the letter and spirit is not advisable as there are many factors which control human behavior. For example, heritage, grooming, educational background company and environment etc. However, those going by conscious could make a human. By and large man is judged by donation, qualities, behavior and nature. In the same vein heritage plays prime role to affect the action of a man. "Baap par beta, tukham par gorah, bahut nehin toh thora thora." Is the metaphor which generally prevail in rural areas. Being a genetic reason most of our actions are inherited from ancestors. To quote we are gifted with their habits, thinking, body structure, qualities, drawbacks and chronic diseases etc. Then comes grooming of the child between 5-16 years which is of immense importance. It is the basement period when we can shape the future building. His daily time table from dusk to dawn should be planned one. He is to be taught about "Early to bed, early to rise makes a man healthy wealthy and wise." He is to be advised about punctuality in going to school, tuitions or any other social commitment of the society. To be truthful, dependable, obedient and loyal, pay respect to elders, irrespective of of caste and creed. Besides studies, he should be encouraged about games with due care to his physical fitness. His unscheduled absence from home should be questioned. This monitoring should continue till the age of 16 years. As regards education he should be advised to acquire highest qualification without caring financial background. An intelligent student should be supported financially even if one has to owe from someone. The primary aim of education should be "knowledge is power" and to gain awareness. The earning should be given priority No 2. More emphasis should be given on value-based education. Special care be given to the company of child especially between the age 12-22 years. Friend good at studies should be preferred. Friends belonging to educated families and those believers of religion should be encouraged as it is said that "A man without religion is living dead and with religion lives after death". Their unscheduled absence from home should be questioned and as well as discouraged. Similarly, company of disobedient, unreliable, drunkard and dis loyal to elders shou8ld also be avoided as they play pivotal role in spoiling the future of a child. Environment too leave a great impact in future building of a child. Elders in the home should avoid quarrel, shouting, and acting irresponsible. Children should be encouraged to watch religious channels where discourses are delivered. Channels telecasting kathas and historical serials also prove beneficial for the children development.

A child by birth is simple and close to humanity and Godliness. His gradual grooming on the lines as brought out above can make him a composite man who will neither be simple nor a complicated one or difficult to understand. However, experience has shown that men having simple nature have been seen in trouble quite often. They are deceived everywhere in this age where shrewd people are honored and receive upper hand. But pure gold has no fear of flames. Hence proper grooming is essential as pays in the long run.

EIGHT

IMPROVE YOUR BEHAVIOR

There is a tendency in general that people keep on saying much more than they act. There actions are far from utterance. They say something and do something. Their theory is fool proof but their actions do not tally what they say. Probably they pretend to be errorless which is not true, as to err is human. Besides they do not keep in mind their actions. Therefore, one cannot call them men of words in general. The reasons at the helm could be various. Of course, to be a man of words is a rare quality. They know that self-praise is no recommendation still while speaking they appear to be self-centric and keep on discussing mein aur mera

i.e. to explain in details about the performance and achievement. While discussing they high light their achievement in a fool proof and mistake freeway. They prove themselves to be un questionable. Practically it is not possible as they bound to err. Thus, they lack coherence between saying and doing. This is because man has committed himself beyond his capacity just to compete his kinsmen, neighbor and opponent probably much higher in status and with better resources. He stores un ending ambitions and plans to start with or accomplish with hook or crook in order to gain upper hand. Thus, with an over committed brain he cannot be mistake free and take right decisions always. There is therefore a need to maintain cool of mind which could be had by storing minimum commitments in order to take right decisions. In case, one sticks to Ashram system of living as enshrined in Sanatana, may be able to go by the right way of living. This is because he will be giving priority to a task which relates to his aashram. To quote priority No 1 for a Brahmachary will be to acquire education and remain celibate. A gharasth to give priority to his duties i.e. to feed, clothe and provide shelter to his family members through genuine means. Whereas a Baanprasti to detach self from family commitments and become an advisor at the time of need. Sansi to remain isolated if unable to go to jungle for prayer. This way your commitments lessen thereby maintain the desired behavior. Self-correction is also a key to update your behavior as enshrined in Bhagwat Geeta (Sermon 2 is relevant in this context). One should bridle his wishes and remain confined to the ones which are essential to maintain self and family. Live in present and remember he is a man and has to become human by dint of his actions or elevate to devas or achieve merger with the Supreme. Accept whatever happens and do his duty with an awakened mind, chant holy name with every passing breathe. Make sure that in no case the treasure (Package) of punya brought by him reduces. Instead, should go on adding to this treasure so that he is elevated. It is the behavior which depicts the real picture of a man. It is like mirror which never tells lie. It will always be presented to you as you are.

NINE
PREACH LOVE

It is said that united we stand and divided we fall. It is also said that "As you sow so shall you reap." The reason of our grief is hatred amongst us. We are after "mein aur mera". In the present atmosphere mein means self and family means wife and children. Parents are being side lined. However, the definition of family could be found in various religious and academic literature. In the present age we do not pay adequate attention to parent and avoid their company and blessing. Thus, we are divided and culture of combined families is eroded. But it is never late to mend. We should preach the culture of joint families and encourage the trend. However, we are still far better than West so for as love and affections are concerned. We act harsh, bitter and become angry with the slightest provocation and expect that people around us should love us. How it could be? You have to extend love if you want to be loved. Love is our nature but we have forgotten it in the present environment. Though Mira Bhai once said "Had I known that love ends in miseries I would have proclaimed far and wide that none should cherish love." But it is half true. In case we plant apple, we will pluck apple nothing else. If you want to be respected, you have to respect others. If you want that somebody should bow before you, you have to set your personal example as example is better than precept. You have to extend good in order to receive good. You have to be pleasant or soft in case you want to have the similar treatment. You have to help others if you want that the people should help you. It is not one way traffic it is vice versa.

If you want that your family should remain united you will have to raise above self and adopt the attitude of forgiveness and remove hatred amongst family members, they are your strength you should try to keep them happy by setting own example anything committed wrong by any member of family should be repaired immediately and issue settled then and there. Any misunderstanding should not be carried forward so that confusion is not added further. In case our families are united our village and city is united and the chain spreads to country level. Our country had been the Guru of the world in the days of the yore because of staunch follower of peace and love and was properly known as golden sparrow. But now a days it is golden elephant, the only thing is that we have to cultivate a vision by uniting our thoughts to stay united, by extending love for fellow beings amongst the various sections of society. Hatred, terrorism, ego and dis respect for the sister religion is the route because of our negative thinking. We are common in shape appearance, size, bear similar color of blood and similar habits and above an emblem of Almighty irrespective of caste, creed, color and religion. We simply differ in thoughts which could be repaired through extension of love. Teaching of Christianity is love as we all are brothers and sons of God. The teaching of holy Quran is five times prayer, extension of alms, observe Rosa and Haj.

Whereas teaching of Sikhism to act as enshrined in Wani. The teaching of Sanatana is to follow rigidly Ramayana so far as performance in various capacities is concerned. Besides, concentrate on Karmas as enshrined in Bhagwat Geeta. Then where is the scope of hatred, violence and disrespect for others. Hence, we should preach love at all costs.

TEN

EQUALIZE KARMAS

Most of us know that the purpose of our life is to achieve bliss, moksha or merger with the Supreme. But we hesitate to take it seriously and join the un ending race of the material world. We can very well distinguish between right or wrong still we go on doing bad for our personal gains despite knowing that these are short lived. In fact, we do not live a planned life. The Ashram system is the best way of living. Up to the age of 25 years one is required to acquire education and live celibate. 25 to 50 years one has to live the life of a garasth. From 50-75 years of age, one is supposed to adopt banprasth way of living i.e. to keep on distancing from garasth and discourage attachment with different relations. Whereas after 75 years of age one is required to go to forest for prayer. This may not be practicable in this atmosphere but at least one can prefer to live in solitude and remain isolated from the material world. It is therefore evident that after the age of 50 years one gets enough time to equalize the misdeeds of child hood or of the garasth done knowingly under the influence of avarice or inadvertently. But we do not do that and are engulfed knee deep into the mire of the material world because of attachment. Even a 90-year-old keeps on running in the race has no fear of his departure. I see most of the retirees having no job at hand join various political parties and local bodies and are generally seen in the hunt of gathering weak point of either of a govt employee or a department so as to black mail or cheat them and grind their own axe. Some people are seen playing at card just to kill their time. Thus, instead of

correcting self and equalizing karmas they waste their valuable period of life which is meant for auditing and reconciling. However, a very few of them join religious forums and work for the betterment of the society. This category is therefore is better than the formers. Majority of us forget our goal and promise mad e in the womb that we will remember the Supreme once we come on the earth. The influence of such request and vows made remains up to the age of 2- 3 years till the child is quite innocent. Thereafter he joins in play, schooling and later in the un ending race of material world and leaves the planet without either fulfilling the ad vows made or the very purpose of human life i.e. to achieve bliss, the moksha or merger with the Supreme. In this material world everybody is in hunt of personal gains through any means whether fair or foul. Everybody points out mistakes of others and never peep into own inner self. Any services being extended to any one bear personal gain in the latent form. Only yogis who do not have craze for prestige rest no expectations. They extend their service free of cost. It is therefore, imperative that one should go strictly by the ashram system so that he doesn't have much load on his brain. Besides after the age of 50 years start reconciling his good and bad actions and start equalizing them by adhering to religious norms. Also carry out introspection quite often so that he could minimize his bad deeds. He should start remembering God with every passing breathe and repent for the sins he had committed in the previous spell. This way with the passage of time he may be able to lessen the burden of his bad deeds.

ELEVEN

DONOR IS THE GREAT

Supreme of all is Almighty which is said to be the creator, omnipresent and omnipotent as well. Next to Him is often said is a devotee (Bhagat), a saint or a yogi who is said to be awakened. But a devotee, saint and yogi rest some expectations. Whereas a donor is the great of all with no desire of a return. A devotee has an expectation to have a glimpse of God, a craze to acquire bliss, a desire for moksha, a desire for merger for merger with the Supreme or go out the cycle of birth and death. Rest of the two, have similar expectation which are their personal and not for the general masses. Similarly present-day human runs in the race of material world to acquire prestige, wealth and various luxuries of the life so that he could be called a powerful man. His circle is confined to mein aur mera i.e. self and family. His performance is hardly different from that of an animal. A human helps others preferably unknown as it is said that true love is that which is showered on strangers. A donor does this job as while extending alms he does not differentiate between known and un known persons. We come across social workers but they too rest some expectations. Thus, any service with an expectation is a business. In case such social worker doesn't have a desire of wealth, they will be after name and fame that too is an expectation. Likewise present-day leaders without a desire for a return do not do any job. Exception may be rare.

To give or donate anything with expectation is not a donation but a business. Similarly, to donate for name and fame is not a donation. To donate a thing for the \sake of gaining prestige is not a donation. To donate a thing to a person who is well of is not a daan Donation, in fact is for a needy. who could make judicious use of the particular item. We have the example of Raja Harish Chander who kept his vow as he had promised to a saint in dream of giving his empire. Karna the great is the top of all donor as he gave his kundal and kawaj despite knowing that it will lead to his death., still he did not hesitate to keep his word and is being known as Daanvir. Another great donor was Raja Beli who donated everything to Bhavan Avtar. He too knew that the seeker is no other than Bhagwan Vishnu the Supreme of all. A donor is great of all as he does not rest any expectation. He never expects anything in return. He is selfless, He acts at par with the saying "Do good and forget it." His serves the seekers with the core of heart. To take care of self is natural but who cares for others is really a great deed. The poet has rightly said that "Apne liye jiyeh toh kiya jiyeh, jiyeh toh ji zamane ke kiye." There is another metaphor "Jnani Jane toh aisa Jan Yaa data yaa shoor nehin toh kahey gowaye noor."

TWELVE

EXISTENCE OF GOD

God dwells in our body as fragrance in flowers, ghee in milk, fire in the wood, sugar in jiggery, as air in the atmosphere and so on, that is why He is called omnipresent and omnipotent. He is there in insets, dog and cow. He is there in plants, vegetable and every living being. God is there in your heart as it guides you, reacts when you do good or a bad act. It appreciates your foe good and curse you for the bad one. God is a power beyond 'Maya' It is beyond Sat Raj and Tam. It is big like a mountain or and ocean and small like an atom. God was seen by Miran in the bowl of poison God was observed by Dhanna Jat in Doseri God was noticed by Bhagat Prahlad in a pillar. God was observed by Sant Tuka Ram, Namdev, Surdas, Sudhama, Veer Hanuman, Jesus, Guru Nanak Dev Ji, Hazarat Mohd and so on. God is in you, if you become dev with zero error. God is in you if you have a vision to see. God is there in a laborer, King, millionaire, beggar and so on. Besides it is a matter of devotion and faith. God is the father and friend of all. God is Generator, Operator and Destroyer. God is there in the Church of a Christian. God is there in the Mosque of a Momin in the shape of Allah. God is there in the Gurudwara of a Sikh in the shape of Waheguru. God is there in the temple of Hindu in the shape of Ram, Krishan, Shiva, Mata, Brahm and so on God is there. That is why there are mountains, ocean, rocks, forest water falls knolls, wild beasts and various creatures. It is there in the air, heat of Sun. It is there in the dune of a desert. It is there in the snow and cold of Antarctica. It is there in the vapor or smoke. He is there in the Himalayan range and the beauty of a women and flower. It is there in the ugliness of a black lady. God is there as the Sun rises in the East and sets in the West. as per the scheduled time. God is there as the seasons change at the right time. God is there as we have the variety of fruits with different packing which are beyond the scope of human brain. For example, orange, pomegranate and walnuts etc. He is the great mater and the creator.

THIRTEEN

BITTER TRUTH

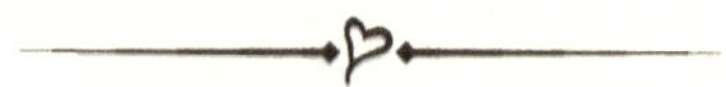

King Yudhistir was questioned by a Gandrav while in exile that what is bitter truth or surprise you find in the material world? To this Yudhistir had replied that a man sees people dying every moment but he never thinks that he is also in the queue. He forgets that with the passage of every moment he is heading towards cremation ground. However, by seeing a burning pyre he may feel for some time that this could happen with him also but when he comes out of the premises, he forgets the very thought. One might have seen on certain occasions when a naughty child asking his mother time and again as to where she is going? When she fed up by the repeated questioning, she says that she is going to cremation grounds (mein chaniyan which challian). Thought her utterance is in the state of anger, but is very true. We all are heading towards same direction. In case one remembers death and God, can always prefer doing the right and refrain from a wrong deed. By doing this he can live a meaningful life. We all are in the influence of "Maya" and are carrying the bundle of our karmas along of many births. Similarly, we are influenced by the environment and ignore the realities of life. We generally remember the God and the time of pain or grief and think about the departure when any one in our locality passes away and we join the bereaved family. Rest of the time we forget this truth. If one keeps his departure in mind, he will have less attachment for worldly objects and try to make minimum use of them. He will act nir-lape with his relations too. He will not have any fear of their getting lost as he will be mentally prepared. Similarly, he will confine himself to the necessities of life and not run after luxuries. He who keeps death in mind has faith in God and loves Him. He will always be calm, cool, aloof and isolated from the hustle and bustle of the material world. He will be soft spoken and has the policy of forgiving. He lives in present with an awakened mind. His performance will always be right. He has respect for every living being. He will be free from ego, anger and avarice. He will remain alike during pleasure and pains. He will be contended and thoughtful. He will preach love desist from hatred. He will care for sister religions. Since our departure is uncertain and we are living in a staging camp, a sojourn, it is imperative that we should act awakened and behave like a human as envisaged above. Thereby making our stay meaningful and festive.

FOURTEEN

WOMEN DOMINATION

In India till recent past men use to dominate. But now a days women have started dominating. The system is reversing by and by. Previously ladies used to confine themselves in the home discharging house hold duties like cooking, milking feeding children and washing etc. In all such commitments which were within the house or at the most taking meals to the cultivatable land in case of farming families. With the spread of education, they came out of the house and started taking part in every field e.g. service, sports, joining politic too. Now they are the part of belt forces in Army and Air force too. They have become bold and started dominating men. We see men washing in the kitchen. Probably it is the requirement of the time. It is said that "A women in comparison to man has double of appetite, four times shyness, six times courage and eight times sexual desire "Going by the saying her domination appears to be to be true, but it has given rise to erosions of values and improper grooming of the child which is affecting our future generation. To a certain extent her domination has given rise to ego as her habit of tolerance and surrender is diminishing. This has also affected affections towards kids. Practically a working has distanced her from children as she is unable to devote desired time with them. Thus, the children most of the time remain at the disposal of midwives as is being done in the West. Children are therefore deprived of desired love affection and proper guidance. Their good or bad deeds go on un checked which is a great hindrance in their development. Their grooming period viz 6-16 years goes on un monitored which is a great dis advantage in their career building in particular and the society in general. Improper grooming cannot produce a good, mother, sister, daughter, son or a wife. In Sanatana a woman is graded as devi due to her multiple roles. She has to be good daughter, sister wife and mother. She has to be flexible instead of rigid. She is required to be of a compromising nature and has to unite whole the family by discharging her duties affectionately. Domination and ego coming in the way will prove a hurdle in executing her duties. Domination by man is a requirement as he is the master of the home. He has to save his family by observing strains of the life as he is supposed to be in the front. Besides he has to defend his country and fight against enemies by joining belt forces. He has to look after his family and property being the head. All this invites boldness and domination. Moreover, his constitution is rough and tough by birth. Thus, domination by man suites his designation and the duties he has to discharge. It is therefore imperative that an Indian women should follow the old customs of Sanatana and be a good house wife first, then a working woman, and then a social worker. She could be an emblem of a devi equipped with reliability, love, affection, tolerance and prove to be good material to keep united our families and save our coming generation from erosion of values. However, the girls should be encouraged to acquire highest education so that they could prove to be a good tutor to their kids if the necessity so arises. Therefore, domination by them should be discouraged so that it may not prove detrimental to the health of our society in particular and country in general.

FIFTEEN

FORMING OPINION

There is a habit in general to form quick opinion about a person after one or two meet or interaction. This opinion may not be correct always as this is formed in haste. Any decision made quickly may not be right. What happens in general that we are born pure and see every other person pious. It is said that to examine gold rubbing, cutting, heating and hammering are the four ways. Similarly, to examine a man his donation, behavior, qualities and nature are required to be determined. Most of us bear dual faces having varied performance. We act according to situation and persons around. We behave differently with all relations and persons coming in contact. For example, we behave with parent and elders in an obedient manner. Whereas with brothers and friends like companions. Known persons in one way and with the stranger in other way. In this situation to form a quick opinion about a person remains a quandary. Same persons have set a few points to judge a person. The first and foremost quality which should be taken into account whether he is a donor or otherwise. If at all he is a donor how liberal he is? Does he extend it secretly or gives it a publicity. In the same vein it is advised that a donation should be made secretly in the way that if it is given with right hand left hand should be unaware. However sooner or later men around may know it. Then comes behavior. This includes how he response at the time of need? Way of taking, how he behaves with parent, elders, neighbors and people coming in contact? Is he proudly or proud less to what extent? Is he a man of words or otherwise? If he happens to be an employee, is he punctual or has no care for the time? Does he pull on with he assigned work or is a head ache for his companions? In case of a trade class, does he charge genuine profit? Whether he adulterate his good or otherwise? In case he happens to be a farmer does he cares for his cattle and feeds them timely? Then come his qualities, is the God fearing and live like a human? Does he live a meaningful life and cares for right and wrong deeds? Is he thoughtful, soft spoken and extent of command over he senses? Does he remember Almighty, morning, noon and evening in case he happens to be a Brahmin? In case of a Muslim, five times a day. How is his public dealing does he extend love to the strangers? What is his nature? Does he extend a helping hand to the needy and neighbors? Is he staunch follower of his religion and has respect for the sister religion? It is said that a man without a religion is living dead and a man with religions lives after the death. Does his behavior commensurate with what he says? Does he care for values? Is he a part of material world or keeps himself aloof to a certain extent? In view of the foregoing forming quick opinion about a person will be hasty and should be discouraged. One should examine a person thoroughly and judge his performance for quite some time and then form an opinion about him. One or two meetings or interactions are not enough to determine his qualities or drawbacks. As to err is a human we may not find a good person around in the present environment, still we will have to appreciate those with lesser evils.

SIXTEEN
TOPIC FOR DISCUSSION

As a matter of routine believing in material world have topic for discussion i.e., they either criticize often many and praise some people once in blue moon. They discuss people around them in order to high light their drawbacks. However, they praise a few seldom. The discussion is so and so has become rich within a short period. So and so is involve in No 2 income. So and so and so is bechara, poor or the like. Many of them will discuss I did this or that if the act is praise worthy. However, at times one may hear that so and so is helpful or honest. Material world discussion make us impatient and take far from satisfaction. If at all one has time to gasp why can't talk about religion, saints like Tuka Ram, Namdev, Miran, Tulsi, Guru Nanak Dev Ji and so on. Why can't they talk about war heroes? Why can't they discuss, donors like Raja Beli, Karna and Raja Harish Chandra. Why can't they discuss about Bhagat Singh and Chander Sekhar Azad. Why can't they discuss leaders like Gandi, Lal Bahadur Shastri Gulzari Lal Nanda and so on? The reasons behind not discussing men listed above will fetch them insipid taste. They do not fit in the present atmosphere. They are graded obsolete in general. But it is not true. They are the source of inspiration and can help a lot in living a purposeful and meaningful life if they so desire. Religion is the way of life and is most important. It teaches you to be kind to every living being. It enables to differentiate between right and wrong. It makes you awaken and remind the purpose of life. It converts you from a man to human. He who respects own religion has care and respect for the sister religion No religion teaches disrespect and hatred for the other It is the man who use it for his personal gain. Saints are the guides of humanity. They are the source of inspiration. They remind us about the existence of God. They teach and preach how to be an observer. They educate us how to bridle senses and confine us to make minimum use of natural resources. They remind us the goal of human life. They teach us to live and let live. They preach love and universal brother hood. Then come war heroes. Our independence is gifted by them. They gave them today for our tomorrow. They rest no expectations or return. They wished that sons of mother India live free They are immortal and are the source of inspiration. Bhagat Singh and Chander Sekhar Azad are being remembered because of their sacrifice. To donate is the great quality of a human. Why can't we remember donor like Karna who kept his promise with Lord Indra knowing well that by donating kundal and kawach he could not survive in the battle field. Raja Beli too though warned by Guru kept his vow of donation. Harish Chandra gave his kingdom to a saint in dream but did not hesitate to forgot it in the day light. They the people to be remembered and could be a source of discussion. Since independence we have seen many leaders. How many of them were clean and honest? Do we remember Shri Lal Bahadur Shastri or Gulzari Lal Nanda They were the real care taker of mother India. They served the country with honesty and without any self-gains. They could be the source of discussion and inspiration for our future generations.

SEVENTEEN

COMPULSION OF WORKING WOMEN

It is said that mother is the first guru of a child. Besides mother plays a key role in making a perfect man, which is true to a great extent. An educated and with sound religious background a women can groom her child in the way she desires. Though hereditary affects the habits of a child but mother can change it to a certain extent by providing good environment and development. Good grooming cannot be expected from a working woman as she is unable to spare enough time to develop a child the way she desires. Time is short at her disposal. Whatever she has it will be spent in house hold commitment. To quote a working woman has to cook breakfast, after finishing her personal commitment like getting fresh, bath, prayer and so on. In certain cases, she to arrange lunch and thereafter run for her duties whether in office, school or elsewhere. Therefore, her child remains at the disposal of a mid-wife, Aya or mahi till he joins a school. The child also gets additional commitment of schooling. The working mother cannot provide the desired supervision to her child because of paucity of time. The only time she has is night. At night the child in general goes to bed early or not in a position to receive required guidance. Perforce both child and mother are helpless. Their helplessness affects the career of the child. A working mother cannot spare the desired time to groom her child because of self- commitment. She cannot educate her child in the manner she desires being an educated woman. Besides she is unable to pass the sanakars she inherited from her parents and the knowledge she gained through education and company. Thus, the first guru of the child cannot deliver good to her kid. More over a working women cannot extend required love to her child because of paucity of time. On the other hand, an educated and sanskari women can groom her kid in the way she desires if happens to be a house wife She has enough time to check and bridle the wrongs of her kid She can keep an eye on the moment-to-moment activities of her child. Moreover, she can extend desired love to her to make him a perfect man. Compulsions of a working mother deprive a kid of the initial and basic grooming which is called basement of human life. In the absence of desired development, we cannot produce good generation. As a result, our Indian heritage is being eroded with every passing day. We are heading towards western culture where value have no meaning. Western culture is far from humanity and various relation are not taken care of. Whereas we Indians have great respect for relation and care for values. Moreover, we have staunch faith in God and its existence. Indian heritage teaches us to refrain from bad karmas and do your duty with awakened mind. Distinguish between right and wrong. But westerns believe in doing without applying mind and repent for misdoing a later stage. An educated house wife prepares her child to go buy our customs and discriminate between right and wrong. So, women education may not be linked with earning that is at par with men but her education be utilized in grooming of children we could produce good generation and take care of values. Once they are able to distinguish between right and wrong, there will be a decline in crime especially of social nature. She may opt for joining service if the situations so demand. But as far as possible her first priority should be to a house wife.

EIGHTEEN

IMPORTANCE OF FOUR

Figure four is said to be important according to the preachers of Santana. To quote yugas, we have four yugas Kaluga, Dwaper, Tereta and Satyug. Their age is defined as 4 lac 32 thousand years (Kalyug), 8 lac 62 thousand (Dwaper), 17 lacs 24 thousand (Tereta) and 34 lacs 48 thousand years (Satyuga) respectively. The wheel of time continues to rotate and its master is said to be the Almighty. Four are the Vedas viz Rigved, Yajurved, Samved and Atharv ved. Rigved is the oldest book of the world. Veda contains each and every duty of a human. It defines charter of duties from a subject to a king. It deals with health care and various rituals of Sanatna. The Indian heritage is vedic based. It is the oldest of all. India used to be called as Jagat Guru because of it foolproof heritage. These are comprehensive and its originator is said to be the Almighty. Similarly, we have seasons for example Spring, Summer, Autom and Winter. March - May, spring brings new leaves and greenery which had disappeared because of Autom and Winter. We come across green everywhere in the form of grass and new leaves. Birds sing and waterfalls give them music. Human being and other creatures feel fresh and energetic. June – August summer brings heat all over compel human and other creatures to be behind the door and confine to their den they feel sweat and tired. However, they gain the last heat of the last winter. Fruit trees bear fruit and other give shade to needy. Sep – Nov Autom is dry; leaves grow yellow and decay. Grass gives yellowish look. Air passing through trees is sound less and does not give music as of spring. December- February winter brings cold rain, cold air, snow and confine human and other spices to their home and dens. Seasons change is natural and are controlled by the Supreme. Four are the stages of life viz childhood, young, mature and old age. In Sanatana we have stages viz Brahmacharya, Garasth, Bnaprasth and Sanyas. Similarly, we have Brahmins, Khastra, Vaish and Sudhara. These are vedic based. Brahmacharya is upto the age of 25 years which is meant for acquiring education and maintaining celebacy.25- 50 years is for those who opt to be a Garasth. They are to live with families and abide by the rules set for a Garasth. From 50-75 years of age, one has to start distancing from families and audit his past performance and carry out introspection. From 75 to 100 years, one has to live isolated life keeping no interest in the material world. This is also vedic based. Then come Pehar viz wee hours, morning, noon and night. The cycle of day and night goes This is automatic and depends upon the Sun rise and set. The duration of days and night vary in Summer and Winter. In Summer the duration of days is longer. Whereas in Winter the duration of night is longer. This system is controlled by the Supreme.Four are the directions i.e. North, South, East and West. North is said to be Dev loka, South is Pitter loka. Whereas East and West is said to the loka of yogis and munis. Similarly Dharam,Arth, Kam and Moksha also count four which are said to be the pivot of human life. He who goes by dharma can make judicious use of arth and will never try to aquire it through un fair means. His actions will be humanitarian and attain bliss with the help of his pious karmas. There may be many more fours which may be a pointer to the importance and might be out of the vocabulary of the writer.

NINETEEN
TRUE HOME

Death is truth and certain. After birth the span of life start counting and shrinks with every passing day. There may be various prediction about the way of life eg, education, health poor or rich miser or liberal, cheerful or rude. All this may come as expected or not, but it is true that he will die. This is definite. For this time and place is fixed. It is also believed that breathe are counted, food is counted, water is counted and so on. When the pyre is lit, one is reduced to ashes and a few bones. The existence disappears and with the passage of time he is forgotten. However close relations do store his memories in the shape of photographs. Kinsmen too remember him according to the thickness of relations, like mother, father wife, sisters and daughters etc. But it remains a mystery that after one's departure. where the soul goes. In this context second chapter of Bhagwat Geeta preach that it never dies. It assumes another body according to karmas. The time frame and process of acquiring a new body and accounting of one's karmas has not the determined. But it is definite that good karmas pay and bad karmas bring punishment. Good karmas bring elevation whereas bad karmas degrade. Good karmas lead to better placement e.g. dev yonis and human taking birth in the families of yogis and elite persons with better human resources. In this context Chapter six of Bhagwat Geeta is relevant. Whereas bad karmas bring degradation and men are put to lower spices (Mud yonis) i.e. like wild beast, dog, cat and creepers etc. Our is a staging camp, a sojourn, still we assume it a permanent one. We see pyres are burnt quite often. We attend condolence gathering too but never think of our departure. We are knee deep into the mire of material world and going on competing our opponents and neighbor aimlessly. There is no end to our avarice in acquiring material things of the world which are mainly concerned with women, wealth, wine, land, means of conveyance and communication and prestige. This is endless and never quenched. This at times leads to bad karmas and the weight of such karmas is increasing by the passing time. Our performance in general is far from humanity. Had we kept in mind about our departure and existence of God, our performance would have been different. Keeping both in mind one deters from bad karmas and always tries to help other being a part of Satkarmas. Besides he tries to distinguish between right and wrong, act awakened, tries to be pious by mann, wachan and karma. Has faith in parloka and keeps his eye on moksha. He knows that his past karmas were pious as a result he had been blessed with the costume of a human. A human will always try to elevate self by adopting pious karmas He tries to cultivate good karmas as these travel with him after cremation. Man is remembered through his karmas after his departure. His material world achievement is forgotten with the passage of time. But his performance and karmas are often discussed and remembered by the successive generations. To quote there had been numerous millionaires in India who passed away but never remembered. Whereas Swami Vivekananda, Swami Dayanada, Gandi, Subash, Bhagat Singh, Chander Sekher Azad are being remembered quite often. It doesn't matter how long you lived but it does matters how you lived. It is therefore imperative that our's is a staging camp and concentrate on performance and try to be a good son, husband, father, brother, neighbor and above all a good human. This will enable one to make his stay commemorable and departure fearless and cheerful.

"Jane chale jate hein kahan dunia se jane wale"

TWENTY

INDEPENDENT, BUT LIVING IN CELLS

We are independent and have completed seven decades. We are the largest democracy. Many of us are under fear phyche whether of death, of being caught because of either illicit or dubious actions or so on. We live in the house like jails. Our actions are confined to women, wealth, prestige and wants which are endless. We are afraid of bad thoughts, telling lie and hatching conspiracies therefore live in the houses which are grilled Then where is the independence? Govt officials are public servant but are encircled by body or residential guards. Their breathes are being numbered and unable to have a sigh of relief. They cannot act freely and have to chalk out their tour programme indicating places of visit and routes as well. They have classified security. Though they are from public and are afraid of public. Do they not execute their duties as expected? Are they not impartial to general masses? Is this a sign of independence? Leaders are public representative s and feel unsafe in public They too Keep adequate body and residential guards. They have many foes in the guise of opponent and public whose aspirations are not met or hurt. They are placed in the categorized security zones according to their designations. They also feel suffocated at times of these guards but perforce have to bear them for the sake of life and the circumstances. They are the machinery of independent India but have to act according to the directions of security personnel. Can they act independent and breathe freely? Their independence is conditional.

Coming to general masses and houses we find multi storied buildings but grilled in our state. May be because of anti-national element, miscreants and thieves etc. There may be fear of death, of being harmed or looted and so on. There may be slight change in the other states but not fear free. They may be afraid of deceits, cheaters, rebels, rapist and so on. They be having fear of death, of being caught fear of losing wealth and prestige etc. Is this independence? Independence was gifted by our patriots after long struggles and sacrifices but we are finding it difficult to maintain it with courage and fearlessness. Instead, we are shrinking ourselves and confined to house because of keeping interest of own families which too have shrinked a lot and are comprising of self, wife and children a very small vision. Whereas in Satana has very vast vision which considers world as family as it goes at par with "Servey Bhawantu Sukhina Sarvey Santu Nirmaya, Sarvey Badrani Pashantu, dukh bhav bavete." We feel unsafe because of bad thoughts, sight or of being caught as our actions in general are dubious. We always try to hide instead of being transparent. This results into fear because we say something and do something. We are black inwardly and white outwardly. We live dual life that is why we are under fear and confined to certain parameters and go on shrinking with the passage of time. Our independence is nowhere all thoughts, ill thinking, ill deeds and ill sight has made us slaves. Swami Vivekananda has said "that everybody is a slave, some are of wives, wealth and prestige and so on, those who are not affected by none are the real human." Thus, one should always be independent, liberal and think whole world a family, where there are no friends and foes and only love prevails. There will, therefore, be no need for the grilled houses.

TWENTY-ONE
PLANNED LIVING

The reason of our grief is un planned, un awakened and un thoughtful living. We live our lives in haphazard and hotch porch manner. We see around in material world and find every one running. We never ask why he is running and where is the goal? What is the purpose? What will you derive out of it and so on? But we start running with him aimlessly without having the answer. When we feel tired and ask the opponent why he was running, the answer will be that his neigh or was running? He too is unaware of the purpose and goal. Therefore, most of us leave this planet leaving no land mark for remembrance. To live a meaningful life same person, charge their battery in the wee hours (i.e. amrit wela) and be thankful to Him. Pray that their day goes pleasant. They do not commit any wrong, kind to everyone, don't harm others and earn genuine money. Be cheerful, calm, polite and come home safe. In case they happen to be a workman, do their job with the core of heart and with entire satisfaction. They are free from anger; store pure thoughts and their performance is admirable. In case one happens to be a govt. employee, he should be punctual and concentrate on job. Frequent leaves should be avoided. Work should be taken as worship as it brings satisfaction. Avoid giving frequents dates to any incumbent. Besides avoid gratification as you are a paid servant. Similarly, a businessman should charge genuine profit avoid adulteration of goods especially edible like milk and ghee etc. Avoid selling duplicate drugs. Avoid stocking of goods, as any act of dubious nature spoils your thinking and brings restlessness Bad thinking will spoil your vision and lead to bad karmas. Your actions start from your thoughts. Pure are the thoughts, pure and pious are the actions. Your vision too should be pious and pure. One should therefore, avoid seeing obscene posture being shown on television. However, programme being telecasted on religious channel like sanskar and asta are worth viewing. These channel talk of vedas, bhagwat kathas, Ramayana, Mahabharata and so on. All these programs remind us about our heritage. Thinking, vision and listening leave great impact on ourselves. Our performance is based on thinking, vision and consumption (Satvik Aahar). It is said that jaisa khayeh ann waisa bane mann." Pure thinking, vision and good hearing will make you a human and by and by you will become a good actor or performer. Besides it will make you a good son, husband father and a good citizen. It is the age of performance and not of utterance as used to be in the recent past. Coming to the titled subject, in case one lives moment to moment and keep in mind above said hints he will definitely lead to perfection. Planned living will not only convert a man to human but also make it possible to achieve the goal of life which is moksha. A human costume is the best of all spices and its aim is not to get involved in material world as is being generally done. Its aim is to get elevate4d or achieve the bliss. Not to step down to lower spices like cat, dog and birds etc. His involvement in the material world should confine to the necessities of life and maintain various relation without attachment like an actor. His life will then become meaningful and worth remembering.

TWENTY-TWO
WHO IS RESPONSIBLE?

We are living in polluted and doubtful environment. Belief one any one has become a gone saying. You cannot trust anybody in general, exceptions are rare. Confidence is lacking in most of the cas3s as everyone is after self-gain. Every relation keeps expectations. Many of us are loose by loin. Shyness, celibacy is diminishing in the women folk. Instead, this is the age of exposure and adoption of Western culture. An age of advertisement. Women advertising for perfumes may be acceptable, but if she is seen advertising with a transparent and obscene posture for a car or a drink looks odd. Indian values are being eroded and the points highlited in succeeding paragraphs may be of concern. Our is an un planned generation. Births are taking place in khel khel mein. No pre planning is done. Couples do not prepare themselves, religiously and mentally before conceiving. They're un known that satvik aahar and to remain sober will make a good baby. They do not take adequate care after conceiving as mother should be free from stress and should see good, listen pleasant and be cheerful always. It is said that mother of the great warrior Shivaji used to listen Mahabharta and mother of Maharana Pratap used to listen Ramayana during the currency of pregnancy. Besides proper care is not being paid during the period of development of a child.TV culture also pose great hindrance in proper development. Teaching institutions also fail to groom pupil properly. There is no distance between a teacher and the student. Moreover, no care is given to the genuine food. Edible derived through unfair means spoil the thinking of kids. Favors derived, gratification, salary taken after rendering less than 33% service is not considered genuine. Money earned through adulteration and selling spurious goods is like poison bringing home. It will pollute your thinking and result in to sickness and many unwanted troubles. Profit earned by selling liquor, cigarette are injurious to the thinking and health of the family members. Money earned through gambling is also not worth utilizing. Similarly grooming of child also matters. To be obedient. respect for elders, teachers, adoption of Indian culture are the key. Be polite, calm, not hurting any creature, thinking every one as friend being the spark of the big ocean of light. Simple living hard work and high thinking. Remain contended as it is said that it is the biggest blessing of the Almighty. Whatever is derive out of adequate hard work should be assumed as the destiny Trust in God and do the right. Believing in "Sarvey Bhaventu sukhina, sarve santu niramaya, sarve bhadrani pashantu, maha kashte dukh bhav bhavte." Keeping foregoing in view one can retrospect that he has believed in "As you sow, so shall you reap." Has he taken care of the planned generation by sowing the seed at the right time and proper development. set the right example as enshrined in Vedas, set the right example by good performance being the head of the family. Had he been true by mann, wachan and karma. In case the answer is no, how can he expect d from the youngsters? We are responsible for disobedience, losing control on the kids. Coming across un reliability, dishonesty, erosion of our heritage, increase in social crime and weak health. We have never ensured about genuine earning. We have been swiming parallel to the tide and never used acumen about its genuiness. Had we put a stop to the misdeeds of our kids timely? Have we not given long rope to them and ignored their mistakes? Have we not tried to make them more comfortable as compared to own child hood. If so, this was not the proper way of grooming. We had been very kind and liberal to them while giving them pocket money, affections and un due previlage which they were not deserving. We are definatley responsible for this weak, unreliable un dependable and dis obedient generation in general. We have failed to give the society better generation. Instead, our ancestors, though less educated gifted better manpower and assets to the society.

TWENTY-THREE

BALANCE
BEHAVIOR

While preaching or making a discourse or dictating someone about the balance behavior, may appear pleasant, a very good advice, but in practical it is difficult to be implement in the state of anger or odd situation. It is also said to remain calm and cool always, it too differs from man to man because of varied heritage, structure, development and the atmosphere wherein brought up. Balanced behavior could be achieved after constant practice and with the grace of Almighty. We in general are distanced from our origin as a result of karmas committed in the repeated birth, we have come from the regime of ananda which had been our origin. As we are in the mire of material world, balance living is a technique or a path which may help us to return to our origin. There are a number of hurdles in the way back. For example, lust, anger, avarice, attachment with different relations and glittering beauty of the material world. Lust is the evil number one which many of us have to face. Under its influence we are unable to take right decisions at times. It incites us to indulge in the evil doing which pollute our thinking. Wrong thinking pollute our actions and we go into the mud of inhuman deeds. It spoils our acumen and decision-making capacity. Saint like Narda could not over power it. It could be won with the blessing of the Almighty. It is a great hindrance in balanced behavior. Anger too plays a pivotal role to pollute the thinking of a common man. In the state of anger, one loses connection between brain and tongue leading to bad or improper utterance which may hurt or appear indecent to the listener. Those having the habit living in present and delay in re action could handle a given situation properly. They can control their anger to a certain extent. Such person s with the passage of time can achieve the state of balance living. Attachment also leaves a deep impact on one's behavior. For example, we see person pass away but we do not make a note of it as they are not amongst our kinsmen or nearer and dears. But anybody who is amongst our relations or close blood related we go into the pool of grief. This is because of attachment. One cannot stop it still we condole for a longer period according to the capacity of tolerance. Therefore, we are unable to go by the balance behavior in such a situation. Similarly, if a house is on fire at a distant place we do not act promptly because of distance or un known owner. But if such house is in our neighborhood or belongs to our relative our actions are prompt and quick. All this is because of attachment. Therefore, attachment too is a great hindrance in balance living. Tolerance and delayed re action are the keys to achieve the balanced behavior. Living in present and keeping an eye on the atmosphere, situation and place must be taken into account while re ac ting. The person to whom you are facing should also be kept in mind while re acting. Your tolerance politeness and lying low help you a lot to win over your opponent. Since our origin is love, compassion and peace our behavior should also be balanced. In case one goes to the version of Chanakaya i.e. "Truth is my mother, knowledge father, religion is my brother, compassion is my friend, peace is my wife and forgiveness is my son. These six virtues are my real relative and rest all is false." It may help a lot in achieving balanced behavior and return to our origin.

TWENTY-FOUR
RELATIONS

Experience has shown that kins men come close at the time of need or with some expectations., doesn't matter who so ever is the relation is. They either take or give as the case may be. May be equalizing the debt or taking a fresh. It is a sort of exchange of favor or money. For example, it may be a marriage, path or yagna etc.

Without expectation nobody comes close. In the same vein blood relation to keep expectation. This includes father, mother brothers and sisters. Neighbors and friends also keep expectations. These relations are distanced if the chain of exchange is broken. Selfishness remains at the helm. However, the relation of mother in most of the cases may not have expectation. Therefore, the relations have become business. A few other relations which are of immense importance are summarized below in seriatim. Truth if made the way of living may prove long lasting. Though it appears at first instant but bring pleasant results after some time. It develops your confidence and keep you stress free. On the contrary a liar has to speak foul and foul and gathers stress and strain. No body trust him. Whereas a truthful person is relied upon and receives appreciations of a number of people. Truth is like mother and should therefore be made the way of life. It has no fear of flames. Similarly, knowledge is power. It always helps you in every field. No body can befool a knowledgeable person. He cannot be cheated by any of govt. official leader or imposter etc. In case one has enough knowledge approaching a govt. official knows the limitations of the person sitting in the chair and own limitations, cannot put off by ifs and buts and has to give him the right answer and his work will be done on priority basis. Professionals like Engineer, Doctors, Professors, lawyers and leaders will receive the similar treatment. A knowledgeable person always gets upper hand. Hence it is like father. Similarly, believing in religion are generally pious and kind hearted while dealing with strangers. They are always helpful and have regards for sister religions. They know that human beings are the particles of the great light which lives in every living creature in the form of soul. They are member of family and are brothers. People extending compassion to others are human. It is their nature as they know that they have come from anand loka. They know, acumen and religion separate them form other spices on the earth. Rest all activities like eat, sleep, expansion and die are the same as of animals. Therefore, compassion in human is graded as friend. Peace is the nature of human as brought out in the preceding paras. By birth everybody is loving and pious and peaceful. It is the heritage development and atmosphere that affects him, which at times distance him from peace. It is like women who is always cheerful, loving and calm. By and large she is liked by everybody. She is therefore compared with peace. Another quality one should have been forgiveness. This indeed is a great quality. He who forgive s is very strong and possess abnormal capacity of tolerance.

To forgive is rare and great act and not every body's business. However, in case of son one acts liberal and very prompt to forgive. Chanakya has therefore right quoted "Truth is my mother, knowledge father, religion brother, compassion friend, peace wife and forgiveness is son. All these are true relations, rest is false." Therefore, one should make them the way of life.

TWENTY-FIVE
DEPARTURE IS UNCERTAIN

People of the material world are generally of the view that they will die on attaining old age. So, they are deeply committed it their day- to-day acts according to their age group. Children are busy in studies. Young men are involved in earning. People in the age group between 50-75 are also committed in earning. Those beyond the age of 75 years of age not keeping good health feel that they are likely to depart and therefore remember God. Healthy amongst them feel that death is far they too are racing in the material world. This is not true as we see that people from different die irrespective of their age. Thinking death as far is not true as it is confined to the next breath irrespective of age. Sane people therefore not forget it. Besides they also remember God irrespective of age group and despite their worldly commitment. A few amongst them opt to take Sanyasa from child hood or from young age. They are the luckiest lot as they intend to achieve the goal of human life i.e. Moksha. They feel that their life span is too short to acquire the bliss. They know that the life is uncertain and unexpected. Death always keeps hovering around and can prick the bubble of life any time. Therefore, it is imperative to choose right way of living so that our life could be meaningful. Our stay here is temporary. It is like a staging camp or a sojourn. Its un certainty could prove to be a sermon for not indulging in misdeeds. If one is sane enough to keep his eye on Moksha, he will always on the right path. So, one should act awakened, remember God and death. Since death cannot be fore said as it is uncertain we should act like an actor and keep no attachment either with any relation or with kanchan and kamani. We should assume ourselves as care taker of our ancestor's property and try to maintain and nourish it with sat karmas. No worldly material or relation will accompany us. Our performance whether good or bad and Bhagwat naam will accompany us. Even our body will remain here and reduced to ashes. We should therefore concentrate on karmas and try to accumulate sat karmas which could prove helpful in the heaven or hell while auditing the overall performance at this planet. In the same vein Chanakya has rightly said that "If body is healthy, death seem far but this is an illusion, death always hovers around and can prick the bubble of life any time. So do not waste time and do whatever good you know. Tomorrow will be late." In this context there is another metaphor "It is never too late to mend." Therefore, we should be very particular about the performance, starting from mann, wachan and karma. Discard evil thoughts, store good one. Be polite and ensure none is hurt with your speech. Indulge in punya karmas. Be kind to persons coming in contact especially the strangers. Have respect for sister religions. Discharge your duties religiously. Make your work a celebration as it will bring you satisfaction. Desist from sitting idle as an idle brain is the devil's workshop Rest assure that you are not abused after departure instead remembered.

TWENTY-SIX
CHARACTER

It is said that "wealth is gone, nothing is gone, health is gone, something is gone and character is gone, everything is gone." It is true to a great extent. Man is elevated or graded from his thoughts and performance. It is easy to quote examples, but to be an example is a tedious task. There are various reasons to possess a high degree of character and an exemplary performance. The succeeding paragraphs may help you to make a decision. Parentage, by and large every one of us behave according to our parents. As it is said "Baap par beta aur tukham par gorah bhoot neih toh thora thora." This is, but natural as we have acquired physique from our parents. It is believed that 80% of the manners are inherited from parents. Pious are the parents pious is the generation. If the parents are so, are those kids. If the parents are wicked kids are alike. If the parents bore excellent character their successors will bear the same. If a father happened to be acting like a bull in youth, similar behavior is expected from a son. It goes at par by the saying "A s you sow, so shall you reap." Exceptions may be there. One has to maintain self and try to remain celibate and restrict self to one wife as enshrined in

Ramayana. Moreover, character of a man is of immense importance as future generation depends upon it. In this context a tale of chhatterpati Shivaji is relevant. Once he was gifted by his subordinates a girl which was captured by them after a battle. Shivaji after having a glance of girl remarked "Kaash meri maa bhi aasi khubsurat hoti to mein be aisa sunder hota." In order to have an exemplary character it is desired that one should have good company during teenage. Company plays a pivotal role in one's development. Company of a saint will make a saint, a scholar will produce a scholar, a player will make a player. Whereas a wicked will breed a wicked. To quote if one takes milk in the company of drunkards no one will believe that he is taking milk. So, one has to choose good company and environment during development period so that he could bear an exceptional character. Child's development starts when he is put to studies. Periodic inter action between parents and teacher is essential to know the performance of a pupil. His caliber and company should also be monitored and judged, Absence from home of a male child should be questioned as is being done in the case of a girl child. Every endeavor should be made to impart the highest educational qualification as it is like kamdenu. Education is the basement of human life. Anything can be had through it, a good job, good life partner, good house and good means of communication and above all maintain good character, provided his heritage is from a reputed family in the society. After getting desired education one gets awareness and understands the purpose of human life ie. Dharma, arth kam and moksha." In this world money comes and goes, life goes soul goes. The only thing that stays firm is dharma." Education teaches one to maintain purity of blood and bear high character. Performance of an individual depict the real man sitting in it. Utterance could be relied upon, may the execution part not commensurate with it. Similarly, thoughts of an individual could not be guessed. But the character of an individual could be determined from his heritage, physique, talk and behavior. His education and company also matter. It is therefore imperative that a man should bear un questionable character, as it affects family, relatives, and above all the future generations in particular and country at large. By maintaining character, one saves everything.

TWENTY-SEVEN
DRINK/ABSORB

By and large we all drink as it is one of the necessities of life, in fact without this we can hardly survive. There are varieties of drinks like soft or hard. Some people like soft drinks, some like whey, whereas most of them like hard drinks. Till recent past women folk used to refrain from hard drinks. But now a days it is gaining momentum and women of elite families are taking hard drinks in open. Whereas medium class women take it in latent manner. Drinking hard by women in well off families is a sign of modernization or westernization we the Indians be modern, but the writer is trying to refer the drink is anger Sane people prefer to drink plan water or the anger. Most of us fail to absorb or drink anger and re act in haste or promptly which leads to complications. Many a times the situation becomes grim irreparable. This is not a quality but a drawback. As a matter of routine to act promptly or in haste is not advisable as emergencies are seldom. One should therefore think over well about the situation and can delay re action until and unless an appropriate response is derived. Generally, our reactions are ego based. Every one of us tries to be ahead of the other and think to

"

be superior to the opponent. Exceptions may be there. Un thoughtful re actions lead to acrimony, altercations, quarrel or fight etc. Sometimes, it leads to court cases which sooner or later end in a compromise. Under the influence of ego, we act rigid instead of being flexible. Had the two of them acted flexible the court cases could have been avoided. Compromising after attending an array of hearing is not a sane act. Acting promptly without applying mind may lead to wrong decision which may be corrected at a later stage. Spontaneous re action especially in the state of rage may prove wrong. As a matter of fact, anger itself is detrimental to own health as compared to the opponent. Therefore, sane people try to remain cool and calm always. Besides they take enough time to re act, so that an appropriate response is derived. Delayed reaction is always right and enhance self-confidence. A man having adequate confidence will remain far from anger. He will prefer to be defensive not offensive. The more you tolerate or drink anger the more you are strong. In this context an old tale is prevalent "A philosopher was passing through a black smith's shop. Instantly he saw a heap of broken hammers. He questioned the black smith that so many hammers have been broken, what about anvils? The black smith pointed towards the anvil on which he was hammering an axe. He further said that it was installed by his forefather which is still serviceable." As such a man on offence will perish soon. It is therefore imperative that man should cultivate a habit of drinking anger and be defensive.

TWENTY-EIGHT

MANN, WACHAN AND KARAM

In general, the behavior of a person is based on heredity, development, education and environment. Similarly, mann, wachan, karam depict clear picture of a man. Accordingly, society too remark that so and so is the man of actions, so and so is a man of words, so and so keeps his promise, so and so is honest and so and so is a cheat and the like. The society is a scanner and keep clear picture of a man basing on his performance. Man acquires 80% of the behavior from parents. Rest of the 20% depends upon development, education company and environment. So, son of an honest person cannot be a cheat in general. Similarly, son of a cheat cannot be honest. Exceptions are rare. It is said that "baap par gorah, bhoot neih toh thora thora." Therefore, most of the qualities or drawback of the father come to the son. There is another saying that "sons of noble persons never dupe anybody till their last breath, that is why kings used to keep them in their courts." Development of a child is a matter of concern. Careful development will definitely make a human. It invites taking care of health, cleanliness, inculcating desired manners like how to talk with elders and strangers? Be respectful to elders and affectionate to the youngers. How to sit and behave with un known persons and the like. At the same time his performance in education should also be monitored by keep periodic liaison with teachers and colleagues. His intimacy with class mates should be checked in order to ensure the type of behavior they possess. This will enable the parents to know the type of company their ward prefers. In case of keeping relations with bad elements, they can timely bridle his attachment with such elements. It is the duty of parent to discourage company with bad people and provide suitable and healthy environment so that they could prove to be an asset to the society in general and parents in particular and not a liability. Proper grooming of a ward will definitely prove useful to the parents in particular and society in general. His performance will be humanitarian. He could be relied upon. He will speak truth and discharge his duties to the best of his caliber in case he happens to be a govt. servant. Being a trader, he will earn genuine profit and refrain from selling adulterer goods, if he happens to be a leader, would be honest and will keep his words. In case he chose to be a religious man i.e. joins the group of yogis, he will attain moksha the sole purpose of human life. Above all he will be one by mann, wachan and karma which is an exceptional quality.

TWENTY-NINE

WHICH WAY YOU LIVE?

Do you believe that God is there. It is a matter of faith, devotion and feeling. HE is known to be the Generator, Originator and Destroyer. HIS presence is felt in the fragrance of flowers. HE could be seen in water falls, mountains, plants and fruits. HIS presence is felt in the changing seasons. Rising and setting Sun. HIS presence is seen in various creature of earth and sea. HE is known as Prabhu, God, Allah, Waheguru and so on. Do you remember him when and how often? Do you speak truth? It appears intricate to be truthful in the present environment but he who determines, it is not impossible for him. However, a negligible number could be truth worthy in the present age. The reasons at the helm could be numerous. But consumption of impure is the main, which has polluted our thoughts. Impure thoughts lead to wrong actions The other reason is" kalyug mein chalta hai". But right is right and wrong is wrong. Are you honest is a very common question for every one of us these days? How many of us are honest? Dishonesty doesn't mean that he who takes bribe is dis honest or he who swindles govt. property assigned to him. He who performs less than 33% of duty is also dishonest. He who adulterates good is dis honest. He who do not keep his word is dishonest and so on. There are a number of adages which guide a man in his daily performance. For example, trust in God and do the right, cut your coat according to your cloth, pure gold has no fear of flames. truth is bitter, those in search of truth have to dive below, first deserve than desire, it is useless to cry over spilt milk, a stitch in time saves nine, nobody can please everybody, it is better to live rich than to die rich, haste makes waste, a burnt child dreads the fire, much cry little wool, well begun is half done, barking dogs seldom bite, a bird in hand is better than two in the bush, do in Rome as the Romans do and so on. Quoted metaphors help a lot in the daily life. Are you able to distinguish between right and wrong? In order to acquire such acumen, one has to go various ritual like introspection, attend Satsang, believe in sat karmas, truthfulness, one by mann, wachan and karam, refrain from criticism, flattery, jealousy, fear and worries. Besides one has to be soul centric. However, it is our duty to keep the body neat and tidy in order to maintain good health which could bear the stress and strain of the environment and execute the assigned duty in the desired manner. Your soul is the nucleus and body are a garment as you are going to quit it sooner or later. Think that every living being bears the same atom of light detached from the great ocean of light and is likely to merge with the same. In this world everything belongs to everybody or nothing belongs to anyone. One has to choose between the two. Extension of alms is a virtuous act which is essential for a human to pave way for his journey beyond death. Both pap karmas and noble acts are carried forward till they are brought to zero either by undergoing rigorous punishment or rewards what so ever in the future births. Virtuous acts not only help beyond death but during life time too. It fetches you the blessing of needy which remove varied hurdles in the life. It is believed that denial of alms to a beggar is a sin. The beggar on refusal takes away the punya karmas of the house owner and leaves behind his pap karmas. So as far as possible not to deny alms to a seeker. A few hints on living a meaningful life have been brought out in nut shell. Though they seem to be of routine nature but are of immense value and should be taken care. Following them in letter and spirit may lead to perfection.

THIRTY

SERVICE OF MAN IS THE SERVICE TO THE GO

There are said to be 108 routes for God realization. In the same vein we find 108 pearls in holy mala which most of the saint bear. Similarly, some say chant holy name with every passing breathe, "as Kalyug kewal naam aadhara simer simer utre para." Other say perform pilgrimage, some say quit material world and opt Sanyas. Other say correct self and become error less, some say go for meditation and realize real "I" {Atam darshan}. Other say performs yagna, extend alms, introspection, join sat sang, go for sat karmas and the like. However, vocabulary of the writer fails to touch the figure 108. The captioned subject is also a way to God realization. In fact, every living being is to be loved as they all bear same spark of light of the great ocean which ultimately merg with it sooner or later. Our prayer culminates with the couplet "Sarvey Bhavantu Sukhina, Sarvey Santu Niramaya, Sarvey Bhadrani Pashantu, Maha

Kashte Dukh Bhav Bavte." Though to be of helping nature depends on heritage, still in order to pave way for future birth and placement one should make an effort of to be kind and helpful to others as the metaphor goes "Apne liyeh jiye toh kiya jiye, Jiye toh ah ji zamane ke liye" or true love is that which is showered on the stangers. This in fact counts towards sat karma and is worth doing. By helping others, one feels morally up and satisfied as it commensurates with human nature. Besides it boosts confidence of a person. On the contrary it one commits an illicit act he feels humiliated at a later stage and his conscious curses. He repents for the misdeed. An act which brings inner pleasure is humanitarian. Rest all acts are influenced by the mundane world and are far from humanity. One who remembers his goal of life will always refrain from misdeeds and keep himself at distance from indulging in pap karmas. His every action will be well thought over. The goal of human life is to know self or God realization. This could only be derived with sat karmas and remembering Him with every passing breathe. The number of chanting should be above three crores. if one fails to reach this target, he can hope for a better future life this again could be had with sat karmas which include service to a man preferably the strangers. As already brought out that every living being bear the same spark of light which a human has, there is no room for violence are hatred with fellow beings or any creature on the earth. Give them a helping hand at the time of need. Mitigate their suffering to the possible extent. For example, if you happened to go to the market, ask your neighbor if he requires anything which could be brought. Similarly, if you happened to go to a distant city on tour ask your neighbor if he requires something from that city or can deliver anything to his kinsman dwelling there. If you find a passerby preferably an old man lifting a heavy bag, give him a helping hand up to the way he adopts the different route. God gives you ample of opportunities to help others, the only thing you can avail such opportunities by helping them. A man often runs to please his blood relations and kinsmen but they never feel satisfied. Come out of this circle and help others, physically, financially and morally, your service will be cherished and you will receive their blessing. Above all God will reward and appreciate you. So, live for others.

THIRTY-ONE
NOT TO REPEAT MISTAKES

It is said to err is human. So, there is ample of scope of improvement or self-correction. Therefore, the behavior of a man should be well thought over so that there is no need for improvement or correction. Even then by and large many of us commit mistakes knowingly or inadvertently. The number may differ from man to man. However sane people keep presence of mind and commit lesser mistakes. If at all they fail to do so, they try not to repeat them. But people at large commit mistakes quite often. There is also a tendency to grade own mistakes as minor and consider mistakes of other as major and unpardonable. There is also a habit of pointing out mistakes of others quickly and give them wide publicity without peeping into own inner self. Since it is the game of karmas comparing self with other is not desired. Everyone has his own destiny that is why we differ in shape. Similarly, we have different names. Hence comparison is un called for. We all are prone to mistakes so pointing out them is worthless. Mistakes like impure thoughts, anger, back biting, wrong vision, wrong utterance, be offensive to anybody, creature and telling lie are the order of the day. Besides criticism, and discussing others without reason is a matter of routine. The quoted shortcoming cannot be avoided unless a man acts awakened. Acting awakened or living in present can be had through introspection, sat sang, thoughtfulness, good company, keeping presence of God and death in mind. Besides chanting holy name with every passing breathe, assuming that we are in a sojourn and a care taker and not the master. This helps a man to act awakened. Moreover, the people who keep in mind that "truth is my mother, knowledge father, religion as brother, compassion as friend, peace as wife and forgiveness towards son. These virtues are really relative, rest all is false." Believing on this saying man keeps himself engage with the right doing and doesn't lose appropriate track, thereby remains far from misdoing. Exceptions may be there. Similarly, who keeps in mind the human goal of life commits lesser mistakes as compared to those who are deeply involved in the mire of mundane world, running aimlessly and competing with their fellow beings. One who always tries to correct self by not repeating own mistakes and taking inspiration from the mistakes of others, purifies gradually. Sooner a stage comes when he becomes errorless i.e. A human with zero mistakes is next to God. This is also a way to live a purposeful life. His future life is likely to be more purposeful and meaningful. Therefore, correcting self is the best way of living as dictating others is becoming a gone saying.